at the

Railing

PREVIOUS BOOKS BY EDWIN ROMOND

Home Team: Poems about Baseball

Alone with Love Songs

Dream Teaching

Home Fire

Man at the Railing

Edwin Romond

The New York Quarterly Foundation, Inc.
Beacon, New York

NYQ Books™ is an imprint of The New York Quarterly Foundation, Inc.

The New York Quarterly Foundation, Inc.
P. O. Box 470
Beacon, NY 12508

www.nyq.org

First Edition

Set in New Baskerville

Layout and Design by Raymond P. Hammond

Cover Photo ©istock.com/FotografiaBasica

Library of Congress Control Number: 2023931134

ISBN: 978-1-63045-105-9

For
Joseph Romond,
my brother,
and for his wife,
Nancy

CONTENTS

Man at the Railing

after a photograph by Jane Tuckerman

I want to meet this man
at the boardwalk railing
who looks out at the ocean
rising like a rollercoaster

on its way home again and
again to the shore. Maybe
he could teach me about love
in this world, why joy

and loss join hands across
our lifetime. Maybe he's found
answers in the repetitious waves,
maybe he has something to tell me

as we both look out at the sea.

The Naming of Birds
for Jan Gebert

I know the ones most people know: robins,
cardinals, and I can recognize a woodpecker
with my eyes closed. But I envy people who
can label the others, those birds from far
away, the ones who drop by for a week

or two just to startle and delight watchers
smart enough to know how rare rare
birds can be. I love the ones with striking
rainbow feathers, but I can't give them
a name, the same for that super cool bird

with feet like red boots. I love that guy
but I don't know his name either.
Sometimes I feel I'm at a giant bird party
and wish they were wearing "Hello,
My Name Is …" tags so I could join

in the pleasure real watchers have,
those who can spot a bird on a branch
or winging on a piece of sky and, like God
in Eden's Garden, look at them with love
then give each of them a name.

At Woolworth's

The counter stretched halfway down the side
of Woolworth's where we'd sit on swivel seats
enjoying ten cent Cokes or, on really special
days, a sundae scooped right before our eyes.

It seemed Mr. Dahl was manager there forever,
his bushy black hair turning salt and pepper
then all salt. Once he reached into his own pocket
for a nickel when I was five cents short

buying a rubber *Zorro* sword but, like
a caring uncle, said "No" when I tried to buy
a penknife when I was only six. I could
do all my Christmas shopping in the squeaky

wood floor aisles of Woolworth's:
perfume in navy blue bottles for my Mom
and sister, a screwdriver set for my Dad,
and *Hardy Boys* books for my brothers.

I bought *Alvin and the Chipmunks* records
there in fourth grade then *Beatles* 45's in ninth,
an official Joe Friday *Dragnet* badge at age seven
and, eight years later, my first can of shaving cream.

Growing up almost everything I needed
was at Woolworth's just a bike ride away
to cashiers who knew me by name, the greatest
store on Main St., the heart of my home town.

Cardboard Box

In Memory of Nabby Romond
(December 23, 2004 – September 15, 2013)

Nine years ago we brought him home
from the pet shop in a cardboard box
big enough for a loaf of white bread.
We named him "Nabby" and loved him
through years of Christmases and
summers, school bus stop mornings,
and Monday evenings when he'd sing
with the fire siren. He ranked last in his class
at Puppy Kindergarten and never learned
any tricks except the miracle of giving love
every hour of his life in our house.
This drizzly morning we carry him in a larger
cardboard box and place him into his grave
we dug with picks and shovels. Loss
covers us like the rain we weep in.

Ghost Show

What used to be the dazzling lobby
of Newark's Adams Theater overflows
now with crates of "Cash Only!"
discount shoes. In the 40's and 50's
Saturday night couples dressed up
and walked through this space to see stars
like Bela Lugosi, the Threes Stooges,
and Buddy Rich live on stage followed by
a premiere film on a cinemascope screen.
Glamor is now a stranger
amidst this clutter of cheap sneakers
and polyester pumps. But behind the nailed up
plywood everything in the theater
is still there decaying like Miss Havisham's
wedding cake.* I've seen eerie photos of the stage,
the downstairs seats rotting from roof leaks,
and the majestic balcony where once I sat
to see *Ben-Hur* is now a sagging mausoleum
of shadows. The part of me that loves
the macabre longs to get behind the wall
and walk among the memories
of this theater. I would point my flashlight
up and down the aisles and see an audience
of ghosts. I'd hear them laughing at Laurel
and Hardy, swooning at Cary Grant,
and when I beamed the light onto the empty
stage, I'd see Bela Lugosi walking from the wings
in his Dracula cape, the Prince of the Living Dead,
staring out at me with his blood red eyes and graveyard grin.

*A character in Charles Dickens' *Great Expectations* who was jilted
on her wedding day and keeps the rotting wedding cake on her
table for the rest of her life.

Why I Like to Read Poems on Airplanes

Something about sky
opening poetry's door -
words above the clouds

The Imperatives of *Wordle*
for Mary

Just six chances
each morning
to get it right.
Green means
correct; gray
means wrong;
yellow's good
but in the wrong
box so hurry up!
Pick another consonant,
try a different vowel.
Come on! Come on!
What's the word?
The sun's rising,
the day's waiting,
your coffee's
getting cold!

Falling in Love with Trains

In the railed world of *Thomas the Tank Engine*
each train is named and wears a face
so when our son, Liam, now three, pushes
a pair of cars to the top of a hill and lets go,
"Gordon" and "Percy" clack down tracks
and smile into his opened hands. This year
our son has fallen in love with trains and
made our den a disarray of brightly painted
grinning cars he's come to know by heart.

Sometimes when I watch him line them up,
his eyes so solemn beneath his engineer's cap,
I remember being his age in the fifties
and the railroad at the end of Albert St.
Locomotives whistled into our windows
pulling cars everywhere I hadn't been,
the nameless places a boy dreams of
on winter nights surrounded by family
and frosted glass. But no dream then

could match the joy of seeing Liam's
cream face blush with happiness
as he guides his trains through tunnels,
over bridges, and around the circle
of connecting tracks until, like family love,
Thomas and his wheeled friends return
to touch our son's emerging life again.

Secret

I hid it between my Bob Dylan and
Beatles records, fearful college friends
might find my *Kate Smith at Carnegie Hall* album.

I shared with no one my love of her old songs
"I'll Be Seeing You" and "How Deep Is the Ocean?"
for it would've been terminally uncool to be outed

as a guy who listened to a matronly lady sing
"It Never Entered My Mind" when Linda Ronstadt
in tight white cut-offs was a carnal proposal

in all my buddies' record collections.
I couldn't bear the astonished derision I knew
would await me so her songs were my secret

in a dorm hall blasting "White Rabbit,"
"Light My Fire," and "In-A-Godda-Da-Vida."
Through headphones I'd listen to

"When Your Lover Has Gone" and grieve
my ex-girlfriend in Milwaukee and believe
in the softest part of my heart that

Kate Smith knew something I felt, something
scorched with passion transcending a face
and figure of a lady three times my age.

I never told anyone what I did in my room
with the door locked, alone with a woman
and the songs only I could hear.

One Wish

for Cat Doty

If a genie from *A Thousand and One*
Arabian Nights ever lost his way
and wound up in our backyard
and we introduced ourselves then
had coffee together (I know this is
ridiculous) and at the end, because
we were now friends, he offered me
one wish, I would ask that time
could be reversed to my son's years
in high school. I'd say, "Mr. Genie,
could you place Liam with an English
teacher who teaches from the heart,
who loves her students, and
shows them in her classroom
true learning is wrapped in joy."
The genie would gaze at me
with kindness, then say,
"I'll send your son to Cat Doty's class,
find him a front row seat and
let his magic carpet ride begin."

After the Play, *The Diary of Anne Frank*

Behind us, the harsh marquee
ignores the sleet and glows its news
in the darkening Saturday silence.

Playgoers rush through puddles
as if they ached to escape the charred
memory of the Frank family. But, for me,

there is no such shelter: Even freezing rain
cannot wash away her face. Anne,
everywhere, all I see is her face.

I weep as I wonder what terror
racked her when Nazi sirens
shattered her secret? What nightmares

did she dream in the box car to the camps?
Down icy Eighth Ave. people pass like ghosts
on a corpse carousel. All around me

I see piles of bones, and skulls, and
cartloads of hair, and gold tooth fillings,
wedding rings ripped from pleading fingers,

and a child's dreams burned to ashes. Her horror
owns me now. This play about her book of days
will haunt me long after this freezing night

yawns into a sunrise that Anne will never see.

Tunesmith

for Jimmy Webb

At age 18 I had never been to Phoenix
nor had I been to Albuquerque or
Oklahoma but hearing the anguish
of Glen Campbell singing "By the Time
I Get to Phoenix" made me feel like
a brother to the one who wrote it,
made me feel he knew the highways
of life and how love can sometimes lose you
along the way. I dropped so many dimes
into our college juke box to hear
the strains of major and minor chords
beneath the story of a guy who leaves
a girl who never thought he'd really go.
I once heard Jimmy Webb at *The Bitter End,*
his voice hoarse and gruff,
his fingers pressing the piano keys
like a sculptor squeezing clay.
At the end he sang, "By the Time
I Get to Phoenix," his head thrust back,
his eyes squinting into the stage lights
as if somehow he were seeing
what all of us could feel.

Breaking
In memory of Hank Aaron (1934-2021)

1953 in Washington, DC
Hank Aaron could see the Capitol dome,
glistening symbol of freedom,
through windows of the café
where he and his black teammates
had just finished breakfast. After
the waitress took their plates to the kitchen
he heard glassware breaking, smashed
so no one else would use them,
so no one else would eat from plates
that had touched the forks that had been
in the mouths of black American men.

But Hank would answer hate with excellence
playing baseball with graceful greatness
through the 50's, 60's and, on one Atlanta night
in '74, did his own breaking, smashing #715,
one more homer than Babe Ruth whose record
stood unshattered for five decades. And
in 2002 Aaron returned to Washington, DC
this time to stand in the White House, just blocks
from that café, to receive the "Presidential
Medal of Freedom" from George W. Bush
and as the East Room audience stood and cheered,
Hank's face broke into a grand slam smile before

sitting down to dine on the First Family china.

Night Ice Skating

I don't ask to do Olympic jumps and spins or
head down, one arm behind my back race skating.
I just wish to stay up 10 minutes on my skates
in the middle of the night down a frozen river
surrounded by trees on shore looking like
bookends in the darkness. Just 10 minutes to do
what I've never been able to do: skate without falling,
my scarf air born like the ones on kids in Norman
Rockwell paintings. Just 10 minutes to propel
myself down a river, my skate blades engraving
the ice, my gloved hands out like a surfer,
a January moon lighting my jubilant way.

Sailing
for Karen Holmes

You need wind
and sun to sail
across water
buoyed by love

of being lost

and found
beneath the sapphire
somewhere
of Rhode Island sky.

I believe God

created waves
for days
like these
when sails

snap

and steer
through air
then
lead us back

to shore

and the love
of family
and the love
of friends

yes, friends.

One Good Thing

It's been a dead parade
of hours since 5 AM,
a march of the bland
with the meaningless and
I can think of nothing
I have done to merit
mentioning or
remembering.

But now, at 8 pm,
I am bathing my son
in a tub filled with bubbles
and blue battleships,
the soapy water over
his Irish white skin
makes him glisten
like a glazed doughnut

and I should tell him
to stop splashing
but this is the first time
all day I have felt like living
so how can I scold
my boy who's found joy
in something ordinary
as water? And when

I wash his hair
with Buzz Lightyear
shampoo, Liam
closes his eyes and
smiles like a puppy

being petted as I massage
the sweet lotion into
his red curls and I know

this is one good thing
I have done with my life
this day that has waited

for this moment
of water on my sleeve
and soap on my nose
to turn emptiness
into ecstasy.

At Arlington National Cemetery Veterans Day Morning, 2002

Across the acres of Arlington National Cemetery
tomb stones stand like soldiers

precise and straight in November's sun. Silence
fills the somber air until one lone bugle sings

across thousands of graves a song of sorrow,
a nation's sacred hymn of gratitude,

as I put my arms around my five year old son
and clutch him close to my heart.

Champion

for Luz Long

I've seen in black and white
footage how you were pure gold
losing the long jump to Jesse Owens,
an American man whom Hitler
called "a non-human from the jungle."
Where in the swastika-filled stadium
did you find the courage to embrace
the black athlete who had beaten you
in front of your leader who
had no room in his life for love
of one so different from you,
his fair-haired, blue eyed
model of his master race?
I've seen the films of you
losing then walking the track
with your arm around Jesse Owens
and his arm around you
grinning like brothers,
teaching Berlin and the world
how one who loses can still be
a champion, can still tame hatred
for an Olympic moment
as Hitler stared from on high
looking stunned and alone
like a demon homesick for hell.

C Major / G Minor

for John Guerrasio

It was our unspoken rule
in high school seminary
to end each Saturday
night song session with
 "Ferry Cross the Mersey."
With the chapel bell just
minutes from summoning
us to night prayers, we'd strum
C major and G minor chords,
their twin cadence steady
as ripples on a British river.
One of us would sing, *Life*
goes on day after day, the
the other would add, *Hearts*
torn in every way, then
we'd blend our teenage voices
like the Everly Brothers to sing
together, *so ferry cross the Mersey*
and always take me there…
This Saturday night, an ocean away,
I take out my guitar and
play the haunting repetition
of C major and G minor chords
and sing again about life
going on day after day, my solo
voice missing the harmony
with yours, missing, like Don
misses Phil, the music
only brothers can make.

At the Teachers' Summer Arts Institute

"You were supposed to bring your own,"
snapped the Teacher Arts Institute lady
when I asked if I might have one piece
of colored paper from her pile large enough
to give 10 sheets to each person in China.

"You should have read the flier they sent,"
she added. "But I thought I was only doing
the poetry workshop," I countered, and she
felt it necessary to say again, "You should
have read the flier, that's why they mailed it."

All around the room other participants
who obviously had read the flier were busy
with their paints, scissors, rulers, glitter,
toward the assigned goal of creating an
"artistic installation with a message."

I had nothing (because I had not read
the flier) so I went about the room asking
others if I might borrow something of theirs
perhaps a magic marker or a glue stick?
All said no and mumbled about reading

the flier as they hurriedly worked on
their own "artistic installation with a message."
"Five minutes!" shouted the art teacher,
"then I will critique your work." I found
a piece of round bare wood from the trash

and a squashed tube of paint that only covered
half the wood. "Two minutes!" yelled the teacher
and I picked up bits of ribbons from the floor
and, when he wasn't looking, I swiped
a handful of confetti from a guy who was busy

rereading the flier. I raced to my assigned
installation spot, leaned the half-painted wood
against the wall, flung the confetti, and ribbon bits
all over the place then with sudden inspiration,
spied an old newspaper in the corner and

threw that onto my collection. It all looked like
the work of a psycho who had just escaped
from Hobby Lobby. "Time's up!" announced
the teacher who then made his way around the studio
making comments about the others' installations.

Finally he got to mine, stared at it and asked, "Whose
is this?" and I raised my hand with the eagerness
of one answering the question, "Who passed gas?"
He kept looking at it and looking at it as I searched
for a nearby window I could jump through.

Then he turned to the group and said, "This is most
impressive! Note the diversification of artistic energy
that permeates the entire installation structure! And
the color! The color! He has stretched the boundaries
of expectation by partnering divergent pigments

all the while maintaining a dominant unity of theme!"
Someone else noted that the placement of yesterday's
newspaper amidst the chopped up ribbons suggested
the transience of time and that lady who wouldn't
give me any colored paper said, "I love the disarray

of confetti, a clear message of the importance
of societal inclusion for everyone." Not wanting
to be left out, I joined in and said, "The wooden circle
is only half painted to convey the existential
incompleteness of contemporary universal existence"

to which the teacher exclaimed, "Oh, indeed! Indeed!
That is cogently rendered!" Then he asked if
I would leave it in the studio so others could see it,
too and I said, "Well, I already promised it to the
Museum of Modern Art but I'll see what I can do."

May 3, 1975

It is the end
of my first day
without a cigarette
and I've come here
to breathe
the ocean air, feel
my lungs fill with life
instead of smoke and,
at Asbury Park,
swear to myself
I will never again
inhale what subtracts
even one future chance
to walk this beach,
see these waves,
and feel my heart beat
to the music
of this boardwalk
carousel turning
like the earth
where tonight
I live.

Seeing *Our Town* in Our 70's

for John and Vera Cosgrove

We are ages away
from our high school class
where first we walked
the streets of Grover's Corners
and have lived decades and
decades of important days
writing our own scenes
along the way. In this theater
we meet again the lives of people
as ordinary and extraordinary
as we are and find ourselves
smiling and weeping watching
a play we first encountered as teens.
In our 70's *Our Town* brings us joy
and also breaks our hearts.
Now we know.

School Lockdown, Classroom Search in My 28th Year of Teaching

After Columbine, before
Sandy Hook and Parkland,
there was the morning
my back door opened
and two armed police led
a German Shepherd
to the front of my classroom.
The dog wore a badge and
a warning, "Do not pet."
Officers slowly walked him
throughout my room so
he could sniff purses
and backpacks. Ice
silence suddenly replaced
discussion of *Macbeth,*
a play where goodness
decays to evil. When the dog
reached my desk, he pointed
his snout into my open briefcase
and froze. The police told me
to step away as they searched
my folders, my pencil case,
my brown bag lunch, and
my pack of peppermint *Lifesavers.*
The officer then shut my brief case
and said, "Drugs and weapons –
we have to check everyone.
You understand that, right, Sir?"
I nodded but grieved for 1971,
my first year teaching, white haired
Mr. Delaney, our principal, his face

blazing red at a teachers meeting
after he'd found candy wrappers
on the hallway floor and gum
stuck into a boys' room faucet.
"What's this world coming to?" he yelled,
"What's this world coming to?"

José Feliciano in Concert

His fingers speed
up and down the frets

of his guitar fast as sun
beams lighting the landscape

of his soul where he sees
each song with x-ray eyes.

That Night on a Bridge
for Gil Hodges

Forget your homers
and Ebbetts Field cheers
from fans who knew
a saint when they saw one.
You can even forget
your World Series ring and
ticker tape parade through Flatbush.
Just remember that night
on a bridge in Washington
with pitcher Ryne Duren,
staring through his Coke bottle
glasses into the water below and
deciding suicide was the answer
to alcoholism. Think of that night
with Ryne Duren when
his fast ball wasn't fast
anymore, the night he clung
to the top of the bridge, drunk
in the darkness, alone
and giving up. Gil, who cares
that you never made it
to the Hall of Fame? So what
if the Dodgers never
retired your number?
We love you for that night
on the bridge when you talked
Ryne Duren down from the railing
then held his life in your arms
as angels cheered from the upper deck
of baseball's summer sky.

Kayak at Sunrise

for Bob Gebert

It moves through water softly
like a raindrop down the gloss
of an apple. In morning's first
light the slender craft glides
piercing the final silence of night,
a gentle swoosh to wake up
birds eager to embrace the blue
of a wide July sky. Solitude
can be beautiful amidst the bliss
of nature's calling her own
to one more day, one more time
in a long, thin boat that's carried
men for centuries and, on this
golden morning, carries one
more on his journey with sun
beams lighting the way.

Boardwalk Love Song, Asbury Park, 1966

After we hear Johnny Mathis on stage
at Convention Hall we walk out to the beach
and feel his last song, "Ebb Tide," come to life

with the percussion of waves a soundtrack
for one more story of falling in love
at the shore. Here my mother and father danced

to Guy Lombardo in the 30's and my brother
and sister strolled this boardwalk in the 50's with dates
who would become their spouses. Tonight I am wading

in knee high Atlantic Ocean foam with pretty Nancy
still glowing from two hours of Johnny Mathis
and, at 17, finding our future in lyrics like *there's*

a place for us, and *the twelfth of never.* We'll eat
at the Criterion, shoot air guns to win a stuffed panda,
have our palms read by a dark eyed fortune teller,

then wait on line to ride the Ferris wheel soaring so high
above the boardwalk we could sing our own young love song
to the Asbury Park sky and believe our voices ignite the stars.

Lou Gehrig Day, Yankee Stadium, July 4, 1939
for BJ Ward

He was scared and did not
want to speak to 62,000 people.

Maybe he felt facing death
was enough to endure but

they kept calling his name
till he stepped up to the mic

and gave 278 words of thank you
and goodbye. His body trembled

as he spoke with the voice
of a dying man still strong enough

to unlock his heart before thousands
and let them all come in.

Again September

for Kevin Horn

Again September arrives shedding
stubborn heat of a summer already
in our museum of memory. Again

we note darkness sneaking in earlier
and earlier, maybe we're caught
by surprise as we were last year

and will be again next year. Strange
how each September seems a beginning
even as leaves die in shrouds of color,

the earth turning orange and red
after months of solitary green. Good
teachers consider the coming fall

a mystery to unfold with students
starting as strangers on a class list
but blooming into learners after weeks

turn to months in the enriching,
fulfilling, sometimes exasperating,
one of a kind story of a school year

that begins again in September.

Hometown

for Laura Boss

We walked the same Woodbridge streets
in the 50's and 60's but did not come to meet
till 40 years later in the warm world of poetry.

We might have passed each other on Main St.,
maybe sat at the same Woolworth's counter
sipping Cokes, or stood in line for doughnuts

at the Cookie Jar Bakery, strangers waiting
to become cherished friends in middle age,
sharing our poems in another century

far from Amboy Avenue and the years
we were young together. Life has taught me
beautiful gifts are worth waiting for:

faithful love, children, and those friends
who make us feel we've never been strangers
on streets leading straight to their hearts.

Eva Cassidy

The years of her life
numbered only thirty-three
her songs unending

Summer Job, 1968

The man who owned the bakery
rarely called me by name, never
returned my "Good Morning," just growled
what he wanted me to do. He often
seemed some place else, a blank stare
into nowhere, and most summer mornings
we'd bake the rolls and make the pastries
in silence. So my last day before
going back to college he shocked me
by suddenly calling across the table
of steaming breads, "Get over here"
and I worried I'd done something wrong,
maybe with that tray of jelly doughnuts.
"Listen," he almost whispered, "if you get drafted
for Vietnam, you tell them you should go in
as an apprentice baker. You've learned enough,
more than enough for that. You hear me?
You tell them you're an apprentice baker —
might keep you from getting your head blown off.
I was in World War II, Germany, I saw…"
his voice trailed off till he said again,
"You tell them you're an apprentice baker"
then he gave me my last pay check. I tried
to shake his hand but he walked away
mumbling over his shoulder, "If they
give you a problem, tell them to call me."

No Hands!

Having lived my youth gripping wood
of a Louisville baseball bat and sinking
my palm into a Roger Maris glove
and loving the feel of raised red seams

on a Spalding hard ball, it was strange
to change to a sport where a hand
on a ball is punished with a penalty.
At first it seemed bizarre, like being asked

to tie my shoes with my elbows but
the beauty of soccer, exotic and new,
eventually won me over. So thrilling now
to see my son and his team aim feet, knees,

chests, and even their heads to move the ball
around a field in autumn as I use my hands
only for applause with my wife beside me,
excitement in the air, the game clock ticking.

Biker Diner Serenade

I thought the tiny tabletop jukebox
would only play in my booth so I pressed G-6
for a cute little tune, "The Unicorn Song." But
its first words, *There were green alligators*
and long neck geese blasted all over the diner
where a biker who'd just ordered the N.R.A Omelet
yelled, "Who in hell played that?" an inquiry
echoed by one with "Build The Wall!" tattooed
on his biceps. Suddenly there was a diner duet
of Fox News on the TV and the Irish Rovers
singing about *humpty back camels.*
It was the fellow eating the house special:
ham, pork roll, bacon, and scrapple
with a side order of Spam who pointed me out,
"There he is, he's the one!" as I tried to hide
behind my egg whites and whole grain muffin
while the entire diner got to hear about *all those*
silly unicorns laughing and splashing
as Noah's ark pulled away. Some bikers
were even moved to prayer and yelled,
"God Almighty! how long is this song?"
as verse after verse blasted through the room
filled with more chains and leather than
an S&M support group. Amazing
how interminable 3 minutes, eighteen seconds
can seem when you're dodging sausage links.
The last notes finally filled the greasy air
and my waitress whispered, "They're gonna
kill you!" so I sneaked out the back door
after pressing G-6 a second time just in case,
to make American great again,
they'd like to sing along.

On My Son's Prom Night I Thin
of *Fiddler on the Roof*

I need to speak with Tevye
and tell him I know now
how our children get to be
so tall, how I don't remember

growing older - when did they?
I see my son, Liam, stunning
in his tux, on his way to dancing
all night at the prom, his time

of SpongeBob and Barney
a fleeting decade ago. I wish
I could sit with Tevye and
ask him what to do now

to be a father to my son
in his beginning manhood years
certain to be laden with happiness
and tears. But maybe wise

old Tevye would just shrug
his milkman's shoulders,
pour us both some vodka,
raise his glass and say

the only words a parent can say:
"*L'chaim,* to life!" and wherever
it takes our children
between sunrise and sunset.

Nixon

In '85 I saw him on his knees
at St. Patrick's Cathedral
looking like a shrunken mole
at Roger Maris' funeral.
Afterwards sportswriters asked him
what made Maris a great one.
"Comes down to learning,"
Nixon said, his eyes tightening
to black, "you could only fool men
like Maris for so long. Keep sneaking
that same pitch and they'll destroy you."

One Night on West 57th St.

Sinatra, alone
with a cigarette
and the notes
of a solitary piano,
sings Jimmy Webb's
"Didn't We?" in the hush
of Carnegie Hall silent
as sorrow except
for the sound of 2,000
hearts breaking.

Coffee Mug

I reach past family vacation cups
from Disneyworld and San Diego,
guitar covered mugs from Memphis,
and St. Louis juice glasses
with the Gateway Arch. But
this morning I need my coffee
from the Yankee mug my son
bought me for a long ago
Father's Day before he grew
taller than I, before his voice
turned deeper than mine,
before "Daddy" shortened
to "Dad." I want to sip my coffee
with my hands around
this gift my son gave me,
feel its warmth across
my palms, and drink the hot
comfort of Maxwell House.
I hold his Yankee blue mug,
its "NY" white as cream,
and think of Liam today
on his first morning away
at college, eating breakfast
with new friends as I stare
into my coffee and wish
two sugars could sweeten
the grief I feel sitting
across from his empty chair
holding with both hands
what my son has left behind.

October Evening

Beautiful to walk amidst the rust
and gold restless leaves dancing
across these Pennsylvania streets,

my Yankee windbreaker almost
enough against the biting breeze.
Something about autumn nights

makes me remember long ago
fall hikes in Cutters Woods
with my brother, Joe, or shivering

down Milwaukee's Wisconsin Ave.
with my college girlfriend, or at
the Jersey shore watching waves mirror

the last light of summer. Tonight
I walk with my wife and our dog
in apple air past an orchard

ripe with fruit soon to be pressed
into cider to sip warm before a fire
wrapped in a blanket of family love

as winter waits in the wings.

In a Pennsylvania Graveyard

When night covers this graveyard
like a shroud and the moon is autumn silver
you sometimes see deer sleeping

up against gravestones, their long, delicate
yet muscular bodies lying like lovers
with the eternally resting. Such strange,

beautiful peace to see them pressed against
chiseled names of the deceased. Some
might have been hunters who spent Novembers

tracking the very animals who now snuggle
like family pets next to the engraved years
of their lives. Maybe deer lie close and

absolve these men for arrows and bullets
aimed at their breed on fall forest mornings.
Maybe bucks, does, and fawns understand,

as we all should understand, the need
to forgive and let go before sunrise calls
us to continue our rapidly fleeting lives.

Sicily

for Julius Gottilla

Surrounded by three seas,
beautiful the way
a woman who's lived
long years of joys and
scars is lovely with
lines around eyes
that have seen a full life.

An island with history
of wars and songs, crisp
mountains, the charm
of late-night Marsala streets
and the pulse of Palermo
beating beneath
the smokey face of Etna.

People speak of summer
heat baking terracotta walls
and its ancient cuisine
of *cannolo* and couscous.
I think of my friend walking
among these splendors
sensing the embrace

of ancestors and at night
gazing up at sky feeling
them bless him in heaven
for the teaching life he's led
an ocean away from this island,
their family love living
in Sicilian lemon air.

The Night My Father Met My Mother

They tell me he'd be the last man
on the floor dancing till the lights
went on, the "Charleston," the "Lindy,"
his wavy hair bouncing, his joyous
eyes bright, a good man moving
in grace across the dance floor.
Through the lens of memory I watch
my dad, honorable truck driver and
extraordinary dancer, one night
in 1920's Rahway, NJ walk over
to ask a pretty woman to dance
and she says yes and he
tells her his name is Ed and she
tells him her name is Margaret
and they waltz to the sweetness
of "Always," the music leading
them in darkness, dancing and
dancing, my young father's arms
a muscular tenderness around her.
Maybe he knows, even then,
he will never let her go.

Final Tour

for Glen Campbell

It took iron valor to go out on stage
armed with only your guitar and love
of the songs you sang. Teleprompters
gave you the words and your faithful
family played behind you to help
when Alzheimer's smothered
your attention. Still, there were nights
you got lost in the spotlight and heard
gasps from the audience when you'd
mix up "Gentle on My Mind" with
"Wichita Lineman" then play a guitar
solo that did not fit with either.
You showed it takes courage to risk
looking like a fool in front of thousands
all for the sake of giving them one last
gift of music. At the end the crowds stood
weeping and cheering your performance,
flaws and all, before your daughter and sons
led you off stage as you grinned and waved
like a Rhinestone Cowboy riding out...

If a Former Student Were Being
Recruited by ISIS

If after all these years you're still willing
to listen to your high school English teacher
let me ask you to remember some people
from our books, the ones we met together
in Room 115 in the days that you were young.

Before you believe murder can be glorious
picture Macbeth at the end of Act V.
Remember him atop his castle,
a man alone with only his evil.

If a masked extremist on an internet site
invites you to his world of hate, remember
the goodness of Jim on a raft with Huck,
or Hester and her crimson letter soothing
vengeance with the power of love.

It can be a cruel world, my former student,
Willy Loman learned that the hard way
and, yes, some live with shattered dreams
just ask Gatsby about that. But I believe
Emily was right about saving one heart

from breaking so I ask you from the depths
of my old heart to prove something gold
can stay from our stories, plays, and poems.
Now you stand before two diverging roads:
choose the path of peace; make all the difference.

Love Poem

She had the face of youth,
eyes as brown as earth
in April when life leaps
with hope and promise.
I thought about the beautiful
"always-ness" of good marriages
as I watched her young husband
lean over and kiss her before
wheeling his paralyzed wife
up the ramp into the van
equipped with what she needed
that day and every day
after the drunk driver
ran the light, crushed her car,
and made Fate ask her husband,
"Do you still take this woman
as your lawfully wedded wife
in good times and in bad,
to love and to cherish
in sickness and in health
till death do you part?" and
he looked at his spouse,
motionless as a frozen rose,
and whispered, "I do and I will."

The Man Loves Coltrane
for Doc Long

The man loves Coltrane
and reads his affection
in a voice deep as a bass note
from a sax in the blue
light midnight show
at *The Five Spot.*

With his whole soul
this man loves Coltrane and
you know he'd stop everything
for the haunting riffs
of "Lazy Bird" saved on an old LP
from the night Trane graced the stage
of *The Village Vanguard,* when

he and Miles and Monk poured out notes
like apple wine. My friend loves Coltrane.
His eyes become diamonds
when he speaks a poem about smoky
nights in jazz clubs and calls me
to join in his awe, to bow my head
and hear with him "A Love Supreme,"
each note a prayer to the God

even non-believers can praise.

Night Sounds

I could almost touch the tumbleweeds
when I'd hear the *Gunsmoke* theme
climb the stairs to my bedroom where
I'd picture big Matt Dillon, spurs jingling,
guarding Dodge City with his six guns.

I loved the safety I'd feel beneath the covers
and though gun shots might ring out,
Gunsmoke would always end the same
with Marshal Dillon winning and Dodge City
safe till next Saturday night at 10 o'clock.

I knew my Mom and Dad were downstairs
and I'd feel the deeper safety of knowing
they were home so I was okay in the dark.
Falling asleep was as easy as Matt Dillon
arresting an outlaw on our black and white TV.

Sixty years have come and gone along
with our house on Albert St. and now
I lie beside my wife unable to sleep
until I hear the purring arrival
of our son's car in our driveway

then the garage door climbing the summer
darkness, our front door unlocking, and
the song of his teenage feet up our stairs
telling me he's okay after hours on the trails
of highways. Our son has made it home.

Now it's safe for me to dream.

When Liverpool Remembers
the Hillsborough Tragedy*

Place a statue of stone
in Liverpool's Soccer Stadium

when 60,000 people sing
"You'll Never Walk Alone"

and be ready to wipe tears
from its concrete eyes.

* 96 Liverpool fans died and 766 were injured in the April 15, 1989 collapse of the Hillsborough Stadium at the match between Notting -ham Forest and Liverpool. "You'll Never Walk Alone" is sung before each Liverpool home game in remembrance.

Flower for a Teacher

in Memory of Father Carlton Paul Brick (1935-2013)

I'm here to place a rose in this room
where he taught my sophomore English class.
I want to leave a tiny flower with a mighty beauty
to honor a teacher who never threatened us, never
got in our faces but did get in our hearts. He taught us
the tragic soul of *Death of a Salesman*, introduced
us to Laura in *The Glass Menagerie*, to Holden

in *Catcher in the Rye*, and opened the door to poetry
in all its splendor and truth. And we learned
how to write because of all his hours of giving
our words on loose leaf his scholarly attention.
He didn't yell, he didn't insult us, he was demanding
but never demeaning and he never let the specter
of the S.A.T. get in the way of authentic learning.

So I've come to this room 50 years later to thank
with a flower the soft spoken priest who asked
almost as much of us as he did of himself and
gave me the model of English teaching excellence
I could only strive for but never attain.
I leave a rose here in memory of Father Carlton,
who stirred in me a passion for literature and writing,

who every day in this classroom quietly changed my life.

Nighttime Radio
for Bill Scurato

Maybe there's some small town radio station
looking for someone to fill an hour or two
in the middle of the night. Maybe they'd be
so desperate they'd let me host the show

I've always wanted to do: play soft songs
by Sarah Vaughn, Sinatra, Ella, and
Johnny Mathis. And I'd read some poems too
maybe Byron, Mary Oliver, or Langston Hughes

plus the treasure of Shakespeare's sonnets.
I'd send out songs and poetry over the airwaves,
be company for lonely truck drivers
on interstates or those holding sleeping lovers

or those who longed for lovers to hold. Mine
would be a quiet show, my voice just
a whisper behind a lighted dial as if
I were telling secrets to friends I'd never know

by name. This is my radio dream, to send
music and verse into the world of night,
and hope someone out there somewhere
might be glad to have tuned me in.

Father Sorrow

Pain
like smashed glass
in my heart,
the price I pay
for loving my son
who had counted
down every winter,
spring, and
summer day
to the start
of soccer season
and stands now
on the sidelines
his face drenched
with emptiness,
watching his team
play without him
as he grips
his crutches like
an injured soldier
on the 4th of July,
alone
with his wounds
as the parade
passes him by.

At the Theater
for Larry and Barb Pargot

The usher points where to find
our seats but once the house lights
dim we find ourselves upon the stage.
Live theater makes us laugh and weep
at what it means to walk in this world
with love and loneliness, connected
to others and alone with ourselves.

Actors speak what we didn't know
were our own words until they touch
our hearts in the dark of a balcony,
where we see beyond the footlights
this make-believe is real, where
we hear the words our souls would say
if they swore to tell the truth.

Second Sun

for Jayne Jaudon Ferrer

It is no mirage or illusion to find
each morning a second sun glowing
across our computer screens. It is
the poem for that day joining
the day's first gold. Praise
and thanksgiving to the one
who makes this all possible,
who sends our daily poem
and proves again each day
that words matter as we sip
coffee, butter toast, and love
her chosen verse, a gift warm
as sun lighting each new morning.

New Shoes and Groceries, Eisenhower Recession, 1958

Recession was not a word
I knew at age 9. I had heard
of *unemployment*, saw
Mr. Salmi down the street
just sit on his front porch
all day. His son, Buddy,
borrowed lunch money
from me twice but
recession was still vast
and abstract until

the Sunday I helped my dad
load his truck and a man
walked in holding his daughter
by her hand and his baby son
in his arms. "Excuse me, Sir,"
he said to my father, "are you
hiring? I know how to drive
a truck." "No," my father said,
"it's just me here." The man
looked down at the floor

and said, "I sure could use
the work, Sir. I've been
laid off from the Ford plant."
"I'm sorry," my dad said quietly.
The man turned to leave
then pointed around the garage,
"I could clean up for you, Sir,
sweep the floor, wash your truck?
I sure could use the work, Sir."
My father answered softly,

"No, my sons do that for me.
I'm sorry." I watched the man
walk out holding on to his children
and saw my dad's eyes darken
with the pain of a brother father.

Recession, unemployment,
just words for me but my dad
could see the man's children's new shoes
and family groceries and the pay check
that would not be there to buy them.

At the Alamo

We speak in whispers.
My hands touch adobe walls
baked with death's fire.

Heaven

It is mid-September, 1989, the first hint
of fall chills the sea breeze that ruffles
my mother's white hair as she sits,
at age 80, in her wheelchair looking
out at the emerging whitecaps.
We are comfortable in this quiet between us
that lasts for many minutes. We don't need
words to evoke the history of family love
we both remember on this boardwalk
along side the faithful Atlantic coming in
and going out then coming back again, always
coming back again. My mother turns to me
and asks, "Edwin, do you think
there will be an ocean in heaven?"
When I answer, "Yes," my mother says,
"Well, I hope it will be this one,
the one at Asbury Park" and she turns
to gaze again at the water blue as her Irish eyes
that glisten now in the summer's dying light.

Amish Elementary School Massacre: Two Poems

I. Angry with God

Females between the ages of six and 13 were shot execution style
and fatally wounded. —CBS-3 News, 10/2/06

The coroner had to stop,
said she could not continue

after charting the twenty-fourth
bullet in the six year old

girl from the one room
Amish school. They'd just finished

recess, maybe they played tag,
and no one wanted to be "it."

Charles Roberts told the girls
he was angry with God, then

aimed his gun. Perhaps Satan
saves words in hell's

dictionary to describe
little girl after little girl

overcome with terror and lead
dropping to the floor

in dresses stitched
by mothers who'd be brought

to the morgue to identify
their daughters, who'd stand

beside a pulled back sheet
and whisper, "She is mine."

II. Quiet Pasture

The West Nickel Mines School, Lancaster County, PA, where ten
Amish girls, ages 5 – 13 were shot, five of whom died, was demol-
ished and the site was left as a quiet pasture.

—CNN, 10/13/2006

Peace now but

sometimes a breeze
leads wildflowers
to dance, their petals
rustling like the swoosh
of little girls' dresses

and then
this earth remembers.

Waking

I needed three alarm clocks
to wake up mornings in my 20's,
each set five minutes apart
to finally yank me from sleep
and greet another day of being young.
There was no space then between
dreams and the buzz of alarms.

But these days I wake on my own
long before I need to and just lie
there as sun erases the night.
Sometimes past people and places
appear like a sad memory slideshow
and I try but can't reach back to sleep
to escape what I've done or

haven't done, people I have loved
and those I had hoped would love me.
Why do they wait until the first hint
of a new day to drag me back
to what I long to leave behind? Why
do some sorrows remain like stains
upon the heart, wounds that wait

for sleep to unleash at dawn? So
I rise early to shave yesterday's stubble,
seek a shower's absolution before
going downstairs for the comfort
of coffee then turn on the news
of other people's lives and forget
for a while the scars that remain in mine.

Kindness

for Philip Levine (1928-2015)

There was just one seat left
in the hotel van bringing us
back to the Poetry Festival
and I was nervous when you,
a nationally known poet,
took that seat next to me,
an un-nationally known poet
hired, not to read my poems,
but to help with parking cars.
What could you and I talk about
for the 15 minute ride? But
you grinned when you sat down,
asked my name and when
I said I was a high school teacher
you joked, "So, Ed, what's it like
teaching teenagers these days?"
and words between us flowed easily
till suddenly the van braked
in front of police lights flashing red
around a deer just hit by a car,
alive but belly-whopping in agony
in the middle of the highway.
The squad car turned sideways
to block our view then a loud
gun shot that jolted me back
in my seat. "You okay?"
you asked and put your hand
upon my arm, one man
caring about another's pain,
the first truth of being alive.

Heartbreak and Desire

for Emmylou Harris

Her voice,
half whisper
half wail,
tells you
there will
always be
a part
of her heart
she unlocks
for no one.
In her midnight
eyes, a darkness
soft as sorrow
lets you know
her songs
hold something
back even
as they give
you more
than you
can bear.

Coda

Asbury Park, August 3, 1962

I am 13 and smiling
in this photo with my father
on his 53rd birthday.
He stands with his arm
around me and I feel
his biceps solid from years
of lifting freight on and off
his truck. My father's grinning,
his eyes bright with life
and behind us the boardwalk
teems with Saturday people.
All around us are summer
and the unstoppable pulse
of Asbury Park in '62.

My father looks like a monument
of muscle, broad shouldered,
barrel chested, not a speck
of gray in his thick black hair,
an icon of strength and health.
No arcade fortuneteller
could ever convince me
he has just four months to live;
that today is the last day
on this boardwalk
he and I will smile together.

Fifty summers later, I touch
the photo like a sacred relic,
the last remains of that day
by the sea, then place it back
in a salt water taffy tin
with a faded post card saying,
Greetings from Asbury Park—
Wish You Were Here.

After Seven Years in Roman Catholic Seminary

That summer

Jesus Saves would blink in neon
across from the flat I shared with
seminarians in inner city Trenton.
We wore black clerical clothes with
white Roman collars and, though
I was four years from ordination,
my first graders and neighbors
called me, "Father."

I loved teaching

my six year olds with their bright-eyed
energy in reading circles, playing tag
at recess, and singing "Everything
Is Beautiful" on field trips to the shore.
I was "Father" to Jamal, and Keisha,
Lamar and Elaine, Tyrone and Niecy
and all my kids who introduced me
to the joy teaching could bring.

But at night

I'd sit out on our apartment steps
smoking and listening to the juke box
from the bar next door. When Bread's
"I'd Like to Make It with You" played
through the doorway I'd feel loneliness
and guilt in my Roman collar missing Jan
in Milwaukee who had just given me
the most beautiful spring of my life.

The music

would make me remember her
and nights of walking the beach
of Lake Michigan or beneath
a County Stadium blanket cheering
the Brewers. Just the memory
of time with her and feeling my heart
unlock to her touch and affection
forbidden in a life of celibacy

made me ashamed

when people walking by would say,
"Good evening, Father." Those Trenton
nights even Jesus couldn't save me
from the guilt of leading two lives
and the anguish of being torn
between two futures. What had been
for seven years a gnawing question
had become a galloping doubt

and forced me

to accept that the brotherhood
with other seminarians
and priests could no longer
be enough. I could not unring the bell
tolling me to a different life of love.
"You can always have it back, "
the priest said kindly when I turned in
my Roman collar. But it was time

to tell myself it could never fit me again.

Balance

for Peter Eibeck

Wisdom is knowing when to let go without hurting,
when to hold on without holding someone back.
I see my friend, Peter, guiding David, his third child,
who sits atop his bike like someone on the tip
of a cliff enjoying the view but sensing danger
in the distance down. And, in the early spring Sunday
sunshine, Peter, who has done all this before
with Daniel and Josh, runs alongside David holding
the seat, keeping him steady as the wheels wiggle
back and forth on the pavement, wobbling so much
David would surely hit the street if not for Peter's
loving hand behind him. But no one grows without
a bit of risk so Peter lets his son search
for balance by finding for himself which is
too much to the left, too much to the right, until
David, whose smile belongs in a museum, begins
to find his center. By June, David will be zooming
past houses with his brothers and all the kids
who bless our block with young life. And little sister,
Elaina, will be waiting in the wings for her turn
to join the two wheeled propulsion of her brothers.
In another spring Peter will, once again, hold his child
on a bicycle until she can move away on her own,
keeping her balance for the road that lies ahead.

On the Day My Father Died: Hungarian Refugees Bring Food

Above the voices of grief in our kitchen
I heard a knock at our front door
and found Hungarian refugee neighbors
with my buddy, Tibor, who already knew
some English. They were crying
as they stood with bowls of *gulyas*
and pastry trays of *orahnjaca*.
They whispered, *"sajnalom, sajnalom"*
and Tibor said, "We are sorry

about your father." Mrs. Tackash
repeated over and over, *"jo ember"*
and Tibor told me, "She says your father
was a good man." My mother invited
them in to join our other neighbors
but they just wanted to give us dishes
and plates still warm beneath waxed paper
filled with their savory and sweet
gifts of friendship and condolence

from the homeland they were forced to flee.
They all hugged my mother and me then
stepped down from our porch and
looked like angels beneath the gold
of Albert St. streetlights. Mrs. Hegedus
called up from the sidewalk, *"Isten aldjon"*
and Tibor said, "It means, "'God bless you'"
and I did my best to answer, *"Isten aldjon,"*
a Hungarian prayer in our American night.

Macaroons

for my mother

If you could have picked your own heaven
it would be here at Asbury Park with the waves'
arched eternity of comings and goings
and that sweet shop on the boardwalk
that makes the macaroons you loved.
All those drives home on Saturday nights
your *mummm* with each bite softened
the Parkway breeze squeezing into our car.
Even in the nursing home, after you'd lost
your appetite for almost everything, the box
moist with macaroons could brighten you
enough to get you speaking about the shore
and meeting my father in '23. Tonight,
the ocean continues its blue journey
and the moon turns other lovers into shadows
on the beach where I hold these macaroons
that I bought remembering how you loved them.
Behind me lights dim on the souvenir stands,
the carousel's circle wheezes to silence,
and I feel what you felt for life's giant and tiny joys
like oceans and macaroons. Somewhere
from the center of the sea's beautiful darkness
your soul blesses me still. I take
a macaroon from the waxed paper
then bite into the warm, wet coconut,
a sweet communion with what you loved,
a celebration of life after death.

Photo of Liam at Age 22

My friends had warned me
how fast the years would go
but still I can't rein in my
amazement at this photo
of you at age 22 smiling
with your pretty girlfriend
on a Jersey beach, the Atlantic
rippling with gold sunset rays
behind you. Pardon me, please,
if I choke up a bit seeing you
grown up, tall, grinning
with your arm around
Amy, both of you looking
so happy standing on the same
shore your mother and I
walked the morning after
she showed me the *e.p.t.*
test stick with its exclamation
of *Yes*! our joy that day bigger
than the ocean you stand
in front of in this photo
I hold 22 years later, your
childhood over, your adult life
beginning with an embrace
of love beside the ageless waves.

Words

for Dr. José Amortegui

They might have been the first words
my parents taught me: say *thank you*
when someone gives you something
and after a while they didn't even
prompt me, "Now, what do you say?"
because I'd say the magic words
on my own. I'd say thank you to the police
officer who'd cross me for school
and thank you to the captain
at the fire house who'd let me sit up
in the truck and ring the brass bell.

I have said thank you all over my life,
for big things, little things and all
the in between things. Now, at age 71,
I say thank you to the surgeon who
bypassed five clogged veins to my heart
and, with his master hands, steered
clear ones into their place. I say
thank you with a prayer for the man
who stopped my heart so he could
start it pumping again with clean streams
of blood giving me more time to live,

adding more words to the story of my life.

Slate Belt Morning

for Bruce and Karen Eppensteiner

The carousel waits in first light to begin its around and
around day in Pen Argyl's Weona Park bordered by slate
quarries where immigrants brought skills from stone and
marble mines in Italy. In Roseto and in Bangor what used to be

blouse mills fill streets with memories of sewing machines
run all day by women under the stress of piece work
and in Wind Gap this morning's sun lights the Appalachian Trail
for hikers on their way to Georgia one boot step at a time.

All across the Slate Belt we are waking to a world
of what used to be and change. Farms from the 40's stand
with cows and corn near huge supply chain warehouses,
national food stores now shadow tiny shops where

you can still buy authentic Italian prosciutto and Johnny
the shoemaker will replace your soles with real leather
and a great story or two - no extra charge. My life
has been here 32 years with its history and hope

it holds each sunrise for one more day of family
for my wife, our son, and me. I wake this Slate Belt morning,
push aside our curtains, gaze out at the mountains,
and call this Pennsylvania town my home.

ACKNOWLEDGEMENTS

Grateful acknowledgement is made to the editors of these journals in which the following poems, some in slightly different versions, previously appeared:

Adanna: "Boardwalk Love Song," "Love Poem"

American Poetic Soul Anthology,: "Nixon"

California Quarterly: "José Feliciano in Concert"

Connecticut River Review: "School Lockdown, Classroom Search, in My 28th Year of Teaching," "Kindness"

Edison Literary Review: "The Night My Father Met My Mother"

Evening Street Review: "At Woolworth's," "At the Alamo"

Exit 13: "Balance," "Final Tour, "Man at the Railing," "Nighttime Radio"

Folio: "Father Sorrow"

Journal of New Jersey Poets: "Champion"

Lips: "Cardboard Box," "Coffee Mug," "New Shoes and Groceries, Eisenhower Recession, 1958," "C Major / G Minor," "Photo of Liam at Age 22," "Hometown"

New Jersey Council of Teachers of English: "Flower for a Teacher," "On My Son's Prom Night I Think of *Fiddler on the Roof*" "Sicily, " "Again September"

Paterson Literary Review: "After Seven Years in Roman Catholic Seminary," "No Hands!" "Coda," "If a Former Student Were Being Recruited by ISIS," "Night Sounds," "At the Teachers' Summer Arts Institute"

Platform Review: "Quiet Pasture"

San Pedro Review: "Tunesmith"

Schuylkill Valley Journal: "Amish Elementary School Massacre"

Spitball: "Breaking"

Stillwater Review: "Secret," "The Naming of Birds," "Night Ice Skating," "Heartbreak and Desire"

The Sun: "Macaroons"

Tiferet: "The Man Loves Coltrane," "On the Day My Father Died: Hungarian Refugees Bring Food," "In a Pennsylvania Graveyard"

U.S. 1 Worksheets: "One Night on West 57th St." "Why I Like to Read Poems on Airplanes"

Voices from Here, Vol. II: "Sailing"

"Lou Gehrig Day, Yankee Stadium, July 4, 1939" and "That Night on a Bridge" previously appeared in the chapbook, *Home Team: Poems about Baseball* (Grayson Books)

"Champion" won the 2013 New Jersey Poetry Prize.

"One Good Thing" was a runner-up in Garrison Keillor's 2014 Common Good Books "Love Poems" contest.

"At the Teachers' Summer Arts Institute" won Second Prize in the 2019 Allen Ginsberg Poetry Contest.

Thank you to my wife, Mary, and to our son, Liam, for their love and support.

The New York Quarterly Foundation, Inc.

New York, New York

Poetry
Magazine

Since 1969

Edgy, fresh, groundbreaking, eclectic—voices from all walks of life.

Definitely NOT your mama's poetry magazine!

The *New York Quarterly* has been defining the term contemporary American poetry since its first craft interview with W. H. Auden.

Interviews • Essays • and of course, lots of poems.

www.nyq.org

Books

www.nyq.org

poetry at the edge™

The Laura Boss Narrative Poetry Award
Sponsored by the Laura Boss Poetry Foundation

Laura Boss, a celebrated New Jersey poet, died of pancreatic cancer on April 9, 2021. In addition to her seven books and her founding and editing of Lips magazine over the last 40 years, she spent an enormous amount of time mentoring and inspiring other poets, often with her good friend and award-winning poet, Maria Mazziotti Gillan.

As a tribute to Laura and in an effort to continue her mission of supporting poets and poetry, we have established the Laura Boss Poetry Foundation. Read more about our projects at:
https://laurabosspoetryfoundation.org

The Foundation is a 501 (c) (3) corporation and all contributions to support its work are tax-deductible.

CPSIA information can be obtained
at www.ICGtesting.com
Printed in the USA
BVHW041954190323
660752BV00004B/22

9 781630 451059